S0-BXV-181

WITHDRAWN

I Am a Good Citizen

by Jenny Fretland VanVoorst

BELLWETHER MEDIA · MINNEAPOLIS, MN

Note to Librarians, Teachers, and Parents:

Blastoff! Readers are carefully developed by literacy experts and combine standards-based content with developmentally appropriate text.

Level 1 provides the most support through repetition of high-frequency words, light text, predictable sentence patterns, and strong visual support.

Level 2 offers early readers a bit more challenge through varied simple sentences, increased text load, and less repetition of high-frequency words.

Level 3 advances early-fluent readers toward fluency through increased text and concept load, less reliance on visuals, longer sentences, and more literary language.

Level 4 builds reading stamina by providing more text per page, increased use of punctuation, greater variation in sentence patterns, and increasingly challenging vocabulary.

Level 5 encourages children to move from "learning to read" to "reading to learn" by providing even more text, varied writing styles, and less familiar topics.

Whichever book is right for your reader, Blastoff! Readers are the perfect books to build confidence and encourage a love of reading that will last a lifetime!

This edition first published in 2019 by Bellwether Media, Inc.

No part of this publication may be reproduced in whole or in part without written permission of the publisher. For information regarding permission, write to Bellwether Media, Inc., Attention: Permissions Department, 6012 Blue Circle Drive, Minnetonka, MN 55343.

Library of Congress Cataloging-in-Publication Data

LC record for I Am a Good Citizen available at https://lccn.loc.gov/2018033432

Text copyright © 2019 by Bellwether Media, Inc. BLASTOFF! READERS and associated logos are trademarks and/or registered trademarks of Bellwether Media, Inc. SCHOLASTIC, CHILDREN'S PRESS, and associated logos are trademarks and/or registered trademarks of Scholastic Inc., 557 Broadway, New York, NY 10012.

Editor: Christina Leaf   Designer: Jeffrey Kollock

Printed in the United States of America, North Mankato, MN

Table of Contents

What Is a Good Citizen?

Your dog made a mess.
Do you leave it?
Or are you
a good **citizen**?

5

Good citizens care for their **communities**. They help others.

Good citizens **respect** people's **property**. They follow the rules.

Why Be a Good Citizen?

Good citizens make a community strong. People feel good when you help them.

Parks are healthier
when you care for them.

Everyone is safer
when you follow rules.

Who Is a Good Citizen?

You Are a Good Citizen!

You can be
a good citizen!
Help other people.
Follow the rules.

Leave things better than you found them.

You will feel **proud** of your community. You will feel proud of yourself!

Glossary

citizen

a person who lives in a city or town

proud

very pleased

communities

groups of people living in an area who often share common interests

respect

to show that you honor something

property

something that is owned, such as a toy or a book

To Learn More

AT THE LIBRARY

Booker, Dwayne. *Grace Is a Good Citizen!*
New York, N.Y.: Rosen Classroom, 2019.

Pegis, Jessica. *Why Do We Need Rules and Laws?* New York, N.Y.: Crabtree Publishing Company, 2017.

Plattner, Josh. *Manners Out and About.*
Minneapolis, Minn.: Abdo Publishing, 2016.

ON THE WEB

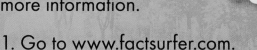

Factsurfer.com gives you a safe, fun way to find more information.

1. Go to www.factsurfer.com.

2. Enter "good citizen" into the search box.

3. Click the "Surf" button and select your book cover to see a list of related web sites.

Index

The images in this book are reproduced through the courtesy of: Dmytro Zinkevych, front cover, 10-11; John T, pp. 2-3, 22-24; Nancy Greifenhagen/ Alamy, pp. 4-5; SolStock, pp. 6-7; Shalom Ormsby/ Blend Images/ SuperStock, pp. 8-9; hedgehog94, pp. 12-13; FatCamera, pp. 14-15; Alfa Photostudio, p. 15 (good); Dobo Kristian, p. 15 (bad); Steve Debenport, pp. 16-17, 20-21; Hero Images Inc./ Alamy, pp. 18-19; Monkey Business Images, p. 22 (top left); Rawpixel.com, p. 22 (middle left); HiddenCatch, p. 22 (bottom left); Stefano Carella, p. 22 (top right); Suzanne Tucker, p. 22 (middle right).